PumpOne®

YOGA

FOR STRENGTH & FLEXIBILITY

DECLAN CONDRON

STERLING INNOVATION®
An imprint of Sterling Publishing Co., Inc.

New York / London
www.sterlingpublishing.com

STERLING and the distinctive Sterling logo are registered trademarks of Sterling Publishing Co., Inc.

Library of Congress Cataloging-in-Publication Data Available

10 9 8 7 6 5 4 3 2

Published by Sterling Publishing Co., Inc.
387 Park Avenue South, New York, NY 10016
© 2008 by PumpOne®
Distributed in Canada by Sterling Publishing
c/o Canadian Manda Group, 165 Dufferin Street
Toronto, Ontario, Canada M6K 3H6
Distributed in the United Kingdom by GMC Distribution Services
Castle Place, 166 High Street, Lewes, East Sussex, England BN7 1XU
Distributed in Australia by Capricorn Link (Australia) Pty. Ltd.
P.O. Box 704, Windsor, NSW 2756, Australia

Digital Imaging by Craig Schlossberg
Photography by Susan E. Cohen
Modeling by Kristin McGee
Makeup by Thom Gebhardt

Sterling ISBN 978-1-4027-5972-7

For information about custom editions, special sales, premium and corporate purchases, please contact Sterling Special Sales Department at 800-805-5489 or specialsales@sterlingpublishing.com.

The exercise programs described in this book are based on well-established practices proven to be effective for over-all health and fitness, but they are not a substitute for personalized advice from a qualified practitioner. Always consult with a qualified health care professional in matters relating to your health before beginning this or any exercise program. This is especially important if you are pregnant or nursing, if you are elderly, or if you have any chronic or recurring medical condition. As with any exercise program, if at any point during your workout you begin to feel faint, dizzy, or have physical discomfort, you should stop immediately and consult a physician.

The purpose of this book is to educate and is sold with the understanding that the author and the publisher shall have neither liability nor responsibility for any injury caused or alleged to be caused directly or indirectly by the information in this book.

CONTENTS

INTRODUCTION

Although its exact history is uncertain, the practice of yoga originated in India somewhere between 5000 and 1000 BC. In Hinduism, it is generally thought of as a form of meditation performed as a path to gain greater understanding of the meaning of life. Western practitioners generally take a less spiritual approach, and usually perform yoga as an exercise program to help increase strength and improve flexibility.

In Sanskrit, the word *yoga* means "union," "bring together," or "yoke." Today this can generally be considered a union of mind and body. There are many different forms of yoga that have evolved over the past few thousand years from countless *yogi* (students of yoga) who have developed their own styles, poses, and flows. The most common style is called Hatha Yoga, which encompasses a number of the general poses performed at a slow pace.

Yoga poses are traditionally called asanas, which in combination with specific breathing patterns called pranayama, make up what is commonly taught to the over 30 million yoga enthusiasts in the United States today. A flow is usually a number of poses performed in sequence using a specific breathing pattern. Each flow will also generally have a particular focus, depending on the poses and number of breaths per pose.

This book provides six specific, graduated Hatha Yoga flows. Each begins with a small basic warm-up flow combined with additional flows that are progressively more challenging. This book will guide you on the proper form for each pose as it takes you through the six structured flows.

THE MIND–BODY CONNECTION

Yoga, in its purest form, was traditionally practiced as a way to stimulate spiritual growth. Hindu priests or yogi devoted themselves to the practice and teachings of this very disciplined lifestyle, with the ultimate goal of self-enlightenment. Over generations, many forms of yoga emerged as yogis expanded the number of poses that accompanied their mediation. Many of those poses were developed through observing animal interaction in the wild, hence poses have names such as dog, heron, monkey, and lion.

With the start of the twentieth century there was an explosion of interest in yoga. Once a strict religious way of life for reclusive Hindu priests, it has now become a common practice in many Western countries. Although the religious doctrinal beliefs took more of a backseat to the physical aspects, the mind-body connection still played a major role.

Today yoga is still considered a form of meditation performed through a series of movements that flow in a particular sequence using specific breathing patterns. Its therapeutic effects on the body, as well as its calming influence on the mind, has made it one of the most popular forms of exercise in the United States. The many health benefits of yoga have received considerable study, and are not just physiological. Increases in strength and flexibility as well as reduction in stress and blood pressure are only some of the health benefits associated with this ancient practice.

HEALTH BENEFITS OF YOGA

For thousands of years, yoga has been used as a means to get more in touch with one's spiritual self. More recently it has been popularized as an excellent form of exercise with a host of health benefits. Some of those benefits include:

STRENGTH AND FLEXIBILITY

Using one's own body weight as resistance, yoga can provide anyone with a great strength-building experience. Many poses require both anaerobic isometric strength along with aerobic endurance not only to get into position but also to hold it. In addition, increased flexibility is considered synonymous with yoga. Improvements can be seen in both muscle elasticity and joint range of motion. In turn, increased flexibility results in even greater strength gains.

STRESS MANAGEMENT

Through its breathing control, meditation, and poses, yoga has proved to be a great stress reliever. From its origins in India with Hindu priests to today's busy executive, millions of yoga practitioners have used the discipline to get more in touch with their feelings. A very successful stress management tool, yoga can reduce pain, lower blood pressure and heart rate, and decrease anxiety and muscle tension.

MASSAGE OF ORGANS

Through its wide-ranging number of poses, performing yoga massages many of the body's internal organs. This helps to stimulate them, increasing their ability to ward off disease and improving their functioning.

DETOXIFICATION

With its positive effects on muscle strength and flexibility as well as massaging of internal organs, yoga boosts blood circulation and immune function. This results in faster excretion of harmful toxins. It also allows for better nourishment of the body by the blood, which in turn leads to other benefits, such as increased energy, mental awareness, and vitality.

ANTI-AGING

The health benefits of yoga are many and varied, but none is as sought after as the power to add years to your life. Although not systematically proved like the aforementioned health benefits, the anti-aging properties of yoga are undeniable. As a result of the stress reduction, detoxification, and increases in strength and flexibility, it is no wonder people who practice yoga are said to live longer, healthier lives. Yoga is said to affect all areas of life—physiological, biological, and mental.

VARIETY

Our bodies are very smart machines. When we need to move, our brain figures out the easiest way to do it. Asked to perform a movement again and again, the body becomes increasingly efficient in the task. Changing the task slightly gives our bodies a new challenge: to figure out a better way to meet the new requirements. Yoga provides the body with new, challenging stimuli that keep you motivated and constantly progressing.

HOW THIS BOOK WORKS

This book is organized to provide a progressive exercise plan. It is a guide to what yoga poses to perform, in which order, as well as when to advance to a new level to keep you working toward a stronger, fitter body.

This book contains six separate yoga flows that vary in their number of poses. Also provided are two tracks of different intensity for each flow based on breaths and repetitions of sequences. Each flow begins with a Sun Salutation consisting of eight or twelve poses. Hold each pose for one breath before moving on to the next. Following the Sun Salutation is a longer, more intense flow made up of a few sequences, such as the Warrior sequence, and individual poses. The beginner level recommends holding each pose for three breaths and performing each sequence once on both right and left sides. The advanced level recommends holding each pose for five breaths and performing each sequence three times on both right and left sides.

The three levels provide an exercise plan, which becomes more difficult as you get fitter and more experienced. We suggest beginning at level one on the beginner track, progress to the advanced track, and then work through the levels, up to level three, even if you are already experienced with yoga. Level three flows can be very challenging and may take some time to master, so don't rush yourself—enjoy the journey.

Whether you choose the beginner or advanced track, try to do two to three sessions per week. Just as the body needs variety, it also needs consistency. Perform each flow a few times in each level before moving forward. Spend a number of weeks rotating through the flows in level one before attempting levels two and three.

A PLAN FOR TOTAL HEALTH

Before you perform your first asana, take a few minutes to consider the whole picture. Performing yoga should be part of a plan for total health, a plan that takes some dedication and hard work. No one gets fit and strong overnight. Yoga is a great form of exercise with many benefits, both physical and mental, but it is not a cure-all. An overall health plan should incorporate a number of practices and habits that have an impact on your body. There are five essentials components to a health plan—strength training; cardiovascular training; flexibility and mobility; a healthy nutrition plan; and adequate rest and recovery. An effective fitness program depends on all five of these measures. The right emphasis on each aspect depends on your individual goal.

SAFETY PRECAUTIONS

As with any exercise program, safety is of the utmost importance. The last thing you want to do is injure yourself while trying to get into better shape and improve your health. When performing these yoga flows, be sure to pay particular attention to the following:

TALK TO YOUR DOCTOR

Always consult your doctor before starting a fitness program, especially if you have or have had a chronic medical condition, are taking any medications, or are pregnant. Immediately stop exercising if you feel pain, faintness, dizziness, or shortness of breath. Wait awhile. You may decide to quit for the day, or resume slowly.

Pregnant women should consult their prenatal care provider before beginning a yoga program. Although yoga has been shown to help with pregnancy and childbirth, there may be certain precautions your doctor will advise you to take.

People with high blood pressure should not perform any inverted pose, as these may cause rapid elevation in blood pressure.

HEAD PLACEMENT

Pay attention to your head placement when performing postures that require you to lift your head off the mat. If you have neck or back problems, keep your head on the mat until you have developed enough strength to comfortably support your head. Think of your head as an extension of the spine, and try to maintain a neutral spinal position.

NECK AND SPINE

Again, pay attention to the position of your neck and the alignment of your spine as you perform all poses, especially forward bends, headstands, and extreme back extensions. If you have neck or back issues, you may want to skip or modify certain poses so as to reduce the stress on your vertebrae.

LOWER BACK

Your legs make up a very large portion of your body weight. When they are outstretched off the mat, they can place a great deal of strain in the lower back region. Your core muscles need to be strong enough to deal with this strain to prevent injury. You may bend your knees in most straight-leg exercises to help reduce the weight. Gradually progress to a straight-leg position as you gain more strength and experience.

FLEXIBILITY

Many poses in yoga require a certain degree of flexibility; some require a lot. It is important to not force yourself into any pose. Never go beyond your limit. If you cannot get a limb into a particular position, it is okay to modify the pose to suit your limitations. With practice, you will see improvement, and before you know it, you will be hitting those poses with ease.

SUIT UP

Wear appropriate exercise clothing that is neither too baggy nor too tight. Footwear is not necessary and is generally not used, especially if exercises are performed on a mat. A mat provides an excellent nonslip surface upon which to perform these exercises.

FOOD AND WATER

It's a good idea to eat something no closer than two hours before exercising. Drink water before and after performing yoga, not during. Right after working out is a great time to replenish the body's energy supplies, while you relax and rest. As some poses may increase the urge to use the restroom, it is a good idea to go before beginning your session.

TAKE IT GRADUAL

Be sure to follow the exercise progressions in this book. Remember, it is not a race, so go at your own pace, taking care not to overdo it. One of the major reasons people drop an exercise program is because they begin too quickly and do not see results as fast as they would like. A new fitness program takes time and patience and should become a part of your life rather than something you do for a short while and then give up.

TIPS TO REMEMBER

Yoga should be a very individualized experience. Everyone will have their own particular goals and objectives. There are no hard and fast rules, rather guidelines or tips to consider:

• Find a quiet, peaceful place to perform your routine. It should be well ventilated and free from dampness, dust, or strong smells. Yoga can be performed outside if the location meets these criteria.

• The best time of the day for yoga is as soon as you wake up in the morning. You should go to the bathroom, brush your teeth, and clean your face before starting. Another good time is later in the evening before retiring. Make sure your mind is at rest and you are calm, so movements can be done with relative ease.

• Poses should be performed on a blanket or mat, not directly on a hard surface. The surface should also be even and clean. For safety reasons, it is advisable to perform your session barefoot so that you'll avoid slipping. Wear comfortable clothing that is not too tight or restrictive.

• Yoga should be performed on an empty stomach. Do not eat for at least two hours before performing your routine. Also be sure to drink water before the session, not during it.

• Be sure to follow the correct breathing patterns that accompany each pose. Yoga is foremost a method of meditation, of which breathing is a vital part. Always breathe in through the nose, as this helps filter the air, and fill your lungs with air. Pause for a second before exhaling.

• When moving from pose to pose, step forward with the right leg first or perform on the right side first. Then move on to the left foot or side.

WARMING UP AND COOLING DOWN

A warm-up is a crucial part of any exercise program; indeed, the importance of a structured warm-up cannot be overstated. It is essential for getting the body ready for activity and helping prevent injury. Warming up before working out prepares you for further activity by increasing the temperatures of both the body's core and its muscles. Increasing muscle temperature helps to loosen them, making them more supple and flexible.

Warming up also increases your heart rate and the rate of your blood flow to your muscles, increasing the delivery of oxygen and nutrients to them and helping prepare them and other tissues for activity.

A concise warm-up should last ten to fifteen minutes. It should target all areas of the body, starting with gentle activity, such as light cardiovascular work. It should gradually increase in intensity, building up to movements similar to the exercises in the workout.

The initial eight or twelve poses in each flow can be considered a warm-up for what is to follow. These Sun Salutation flows start you off at a slower pace and gradually get you ready to perform the more demanding exercises that follow.

Just as important as warming up before exercising is a good cool-down afterward. Cooling down helps return your core temperature to normal and allows muscles to relax and return to their original length. At the end of each flow there is the Corpse Pose, or Savasana, which serves to clear the mind and allow the body to completely relax.

Savasana is widely regarded as the most important pose in yoga, as it is the time you take to relax and recover from the more strenuous poses you have just completed. Take the opportunity to really focus on that mind-body connection. Relax your breathing and clear your mind. Let your body focus on regeneration.

#1 MOUNTAIN POSE TO REACH UP

(TADASANA TO URDHVA HASTASANA)

MOUNTAIN POSE

- Stand upright, looking straight ahead, with your hands by your sides and your feet firmly planted on the mat.

- Lift your abdomen in and upward.

- Your weight should be balanced evenly on both feet.

REACH UP

- Raise your hands together above your head, and look straight up.

- Keep your shoulders from lifting and your ribs from jutting out.

- Hug your elbows toward the midline.

BEGINNER	ADVANCED
Hold each pose for 1 breath.	Hold each pose for 1 breath.

#2 STANDING FORWARD BEND
(UTTANASANA)

- Bend forward from the hips, keeping your legs straight.

- Lower your torso down to rest your head on your shins, lengthening your spine.

- Place your hands flat on the floor beside your feet.

- If you cannot perform the movement with your legs straight, bend your knees slightly.

BEGINNER	ADVANCED
Hold the pose for 1 breath.	Hold the pose for 1 breath.

#3 CRESCENT LUNGE

(ANJANEYASANA)

- Step backward until your back knee and the top of your foot touch the floor.

- Bend the front knee, pressing firmly through the heel while keeping your hips level.

- Raise your arms straight above your head, bringing your palms together, and slightly arch your back.

- Look up at your fingers.

BEGINNER	ADVANCED
Hold the pose for 1 breath. Perform this pose once on each side.	Hold the pose for 1 breath. Perform this pose once on each side.

#4 PLANK

- Take a step back with the bent leg, and lower your body toward the floor until your shoulders are directly over your hands.

- Your body should be completely straight from heels to head.

- Look down at the floor, keeping your head in line with your spine.

BEGINNER	ADVANCED
Hold the pose for 1 breath.	Hold the pose for 1 breath.

KNEES CHEST CHIN

- From Plank position, lower your knees to the floor, followed by your chest and chin.

- Make sure your elbows bend straight back, not to the sides.

- Keep a slight arch in your lower back, with your abdomen held in.

BABY COBRA

- From the Knees Chest Chin pose, slide forward onto your belly and point your toes, keeping the tops of your feet on the mat.

- Pull your shoulders back, opening your chest, and gaze down the tip of your nose.

BEGINNER	ADVANCED
Hold each pose for 1 breath.	Hold each pose for 1 breath.

#6 DOWNWARD FACING DOG
(ADHO MUKHA SVANASANA)

- Push back with your hands and raise your hips high into the air.

- Straighten your legs and lengthen your heels toward the floor.

- Lengthen your spine, and look toward your navel.

- Your hands should be in front of your shoulders, with your fingers spread.

BEGINNER	ADVANCED
Hold the pose for 1 breath.	Hold the pose for 1 breath.

#7 CRESCENT LUNGE

(ANJANEYASANA)

- Step one leg forward into a lunge, bending your front knee and pressing firmly through your heel. Keep your hips level while dropping your back knee to the floor.

- Raise your arms straight above your head, bringing your palms together, and slightly arch your back.

- Look up at your fingers.

BEGINNER	ADVANCED
Hold the pose for 1 breath. Perform this pose once on each side.	Hold the pose for 1 breath. Perform this pose once on each side.

#8 STANDING FORWARD BEND

(UTTANASANA)

- Step forward, bringing your feet together.

- Bend forward from the hips, keeping your legs straight.

- Fold into your legs to rest your head on your shins, lengthening your spine.

- Place your hands flat on the floor beside your feet.

- If you cannot perform the pose with your legs straight, bend your knees slightly.

BEGINNER	ADVANCED
Hold the pose for 1 breath.	Hold the pose for 1 breath.

#9 REACH UP TO MOUNTAIN POSE

(URDHVA HASTASANA TO TADASANA)

REACH UP

- Return to an upright position, and raise your hands together above your head, looking straight up.

- Keep your shoulders from lifting and your ribs from jutting out.

- Hug your elbows toward the midline.

MOUNTAIN POSE

- Lower your arms back by your sides, and look straight ahead, with your feet firmly planted.

- Lift your abdomen in and upward.

- Your weight should be balanced evenly on the feet.

BEGINNER	ADVANCED
Hold each pose for 1 breath.	Hold each pose for 1 breath.

#10 HIGH LUNGE

- Step backward, straightening your back leg.

- Keep your torso upright while bending the knee of your front leg and pressing firmly through the heel, keeping your hips level.

- Raise your arms straight overhead, maintaining a neutral spine and looking straight ahead.

- Keep the knee of your lead foot directly over the ankle.

BEGINNER	ADVANCED
Hold the pose for 3 breaths. Perform this pose once on each side.	Hold the pose for 5 breaths. Perform this pose 3 times on each side.

#11 EAGLE POSE

(GARUDASANA)

- Step back to an upright position, slightly bend your knees, and lift your right foot to cross your right thigh over your left leg and hook your foot behind the lower calf.

- Wrap your right arm on top of your left, bending your elbows and raising your forearms straight up.

- The palms of your hands should be touching.

BEGINNER	ADVANCED
Hold the pose for 3 breaths. Perform this pose once on each side.	Hold the pose for 5 breaths. Perform this pose 3 times on each side.

#12 STANDING FORWARD BEND
(UTTANASANA)

- Stand upright, with your feet about hip-width apart.

- Inhale and bend forward from the hips, keeping your legs straight and your feet apart.

- Lower your torso down to rest your head on your shins, lengthening your spine.

- Hold your big toes or grab your ankles from behind, with your elbows bent.

- If you cannot perform the pose with your legs straight, bend your knees slightly.

BEGINNER	ADVANCED
Hold the pose for 3 breaths.	Hold the pose for 5 breaths.

#13 COBBLER'S POSE

(BADDHA KONASANA)

- Sit with your legs extended straight out in front of you.

- Bend your knees, and pull your heels toward your pelvis.

- Lower your knees out to the sides, and bring the soles of your feet together.

- Bend forward from the hips, and lower your head to your feet.

LEVEL 1: FLOW 1

BEGINNER	ADVANCED
Hold the pose for 3 breaths.	Hold the pose for 5 breaths.

#14 BOAT POSE
(NAVASANA)

BEGINNER	ADVANCED
Hold the pose for 3 breaths.	Hold the pose for 5 breaths.

- Straighten your legs back out in front, with your arms by your sides.

- Bend your knees, and lift your feet off the floor.

- Lean back slightly as you raise and straighten your legs.

- Bring your arms up straight until they are parallel with the floor.

- Keep your chest up, and do not round your lower back. Stay long in the spine.

(UPAVISTHA KONASANA)

- Lower your legs back to the floor, and straighten them out in front of you.

- Slowly open your legs straight out to the sides. Keep your feet and knees pointing to the ceiling.

- Bend forward from your hips, and reach your hands toward your feet.

- Lengthen out from your lower back.

BEGINNER	ADVANCED
Hold the pose for 3 breaths.	Hold the pose for 5 breaths.

#16 TABLE TOP

- Bring your legs back to the front, placing your feet flat on the mat with your knees bent.

- Put your hands slightly behind your buttocks and directly below your shoulders, with your fingers pointing forward.

- Lift your torso up off the floor, using both your arms and legs, and ending in a straight position.

- Keep your hands below your shoulders and your knees over your ankles.

- Let your head drop back if you find that comfortable.

BEGINNER	ADVANCED
Hold the pose for 3 breaths.	Hold the pose for 5 breaths.

(HALASANA)

- Lower your body back to the mat, with your knees bent, your feet flat, and your arms by your sides.

- Exhale, bringing your knees to your chest, and press your arms into the floor.

- Straighten your legs, and lower them back behind your head while keeping them straight.

- Touch your feet to the floor.

- Bring your hands together, with your arms straight behind your back.

BEGINNER	ADVANCED
Hold the pose for 3 breaths.	Hold the pose for 5 breaths.

#18 RECLINED TWISTS TO CORPSE POSE

(RECLINED TWISTS TO SAVASANA)

RECLINED TWISTS

- Return to lie on your back with your knees bent, your feet flat, and your arms by your sides.

- Bring your knees into your chest, and then slowly lower them down to one side.

- Place your hand on your top knee to help ease your legs to the floor.

- Turn your head to the opposite side, and look toward the fingers of your outstretched arm.

CORPSE POSE

- Lie flat on your back on the mat, with your legs slightly apart and your arms stretched out by your sides, palms up.

- Close your eyes and relax your breathing, letting go of any tension.

BEGINNER	ADVANCED
Hold Reclined Twists for 3 breaths. Perform Reclined Twists once on each side before performing Corpse Pose. Hold Corpse Pose for a few minutes.	Hold Reclined Twists for 5 breaths. Perform Reclined Twists 3 times on each side before performing Corpse Pose. Hold Corpse Pose for a few minutes.

#13 WARRIOR SEQUENCE

(VIRABHADRASANA SEQUENCE)

Perform the first twelve poses from Level 1, Flow 1 (pages 13–24), before moving on to these new poses.

WARRIOR I

- Step one leg back about 4 feet, and turn the foot out slightly.

- Raise your arms straight overhead, pressing your palms together, and look up at your fingers.

- Bend your front knee so it is directly over your ankle. Ground your back heel into the floor and keep your hips facing forward.

WARRIOR II

- Lower your arms until they are parallel with the floor, with your palms down, and reach out to both sides.

- Open your torso to the side and turn your head to look forward along your arm.

WARRIOR III

- Step forward onto your front leg, lengthening your torso to bend forward until your torso is parallel to the floor.

- Lift your back leg up behind you and bring your arms up by your sides.

- Keep your hips level, and lift your ribs away from the floor, reaching through the raised leg behind you.

- Your head and neck should be straight and in line with your torso.

BEGINNER	ADVANCED
Hold each pose for 3 breaths. Perform this sequence once on each side.	Hold each pose for 5 breaths. Perform this sequence 3 times on each side.

#14 TREE POSE
(VRKSASANA)

- Stand upright and raise one leg, bending it at the knee and placing the sole your foot on the inside of your other thigh.

- Bring your palms together in front of your chest.

- Stay grounded through the entire foot of the standing leg.

- Look straight ahead, and focus on your breathing.

BEGINNER	ADVANCED
Hold the pose for 3 breaths. Perform this pose once on each side.	Hold the pose for 5 breaths. Perform this pose 3 times on each side.

#15 TRIANGLE POSE TO EXTENDED ANGLE

(TRIKONASANA TO PARSVOTTANASANA)

TRIANGLE POSE

- Return to an upright position, with your arms by your sides.

- Step apart one leg-length, turning your front foot outward 90 degrees to the side and your back foot inward 75 degrees.

- Lower your hand to the floor, behind your front foot, and stretch your other hand toward the ceiling, keeping it in line with your hand on the floor.

- Make sure to lengthen through both sides of your waist.

EXTENDED ANGLE

- From Triangle Pose, bend your front knee and rest your lower elbow on this knee.

- Stretch your other arm over your head as you extend over to the side of the front foot.

- Look up to the ceiling, keeping your shoulders relaxed.

- Try to form a straight line from the back foot out to the tops of the fingers above.

BEGINNER	ADVANCED
Hold each pose for 3 breaths. Perform this sequence once on each side.	Hold the each for 5 breaths. Perform this sequence 3 times on each side.

#16 WIDE LEG FORWARD BEND

(PRASARITA PADOTTANASANA)

- From an upright position, spread your legs about 4 feet apart.

- Place your hands on your hips and inhale.

- Press firmly through the outer edges of your feet, lifting your inner arches.

- Exhale, and bend forward at the hips.

- Lower your head and hands to the floor, placing your hands directly below your shoulders with your elbows bent behind you.

BEGINNER	ADVANCED
Hold the pose for 3 breaths.	Hold the pose for 5 breaths.

#17 SEATED FORWARD BEND

(PASCHIMOTTANASANA)

- Sit on the floor, with your legs straight out in front of you, and hold your big toes.

- Bend forward at the hips, and lower your head toward your knees.

- Gently pull your big toes toward your head.

- Stay centered on your sit bones (the bones you sit on).

- Lengthen your spine, and keep your feet flexed.

LEVEL 1: FLOW 2

BEGINNER	ADVANCED
Hold the pose for 3 breaths.	Hold the pose for 5 breaths.

#18 HEAD TO KNEE
(PARIVRTTA JANU SIRSASANA)

- Sit back upright, and bend one knee into your chest. Place the sole of your foot into the opposite inner thigh as you turn the leg out from the hip joint.

- Bend forward at the hips, and lower your head toward your straight knee.

- Reach your hands to your outstretched foot, clasping it if possible.

- Stay centered on your sit bones.

- Lengthen your spine, and keep your foot flexed.

BEGINNER	ADVANCED
Hold the pose for 3 breaths.	Hold the pose for 5 breaths.

(SETU BANDHASANA)

- Lie flat on your back, with your knees bent, your feet flat on the mat and slightly apart, and your arms by your sides.

- Inhale and lift your hips off the floor, rolling up onto your shoulders into a back bend.

- Bring your arms straight under your torso, clasping your hands together between your feet.

BEGINNER	ADVANCED
Hold the pose for 3 breaths.	Hold the pose for 5 breaths.

#20 RECLINED TWISTS TO CORPSE POSE

(RECLINED TWISTS TO SAVASANA)

RECLINED TWISTS

- Lower yourself back to the floor, and lie on your back with your legs straight and your arms stretched out to the sides.

- Bring one knee into your chest, and then slowly lower it down to the opposite side while keeping your other leg straight.

- Place your hand on this bent knee to help ease your leg to the floor.

- Turn your head to the opposite side, and look toward the fingers of your outstretched arm.

CORPSE POSE

- Lie flat on your back on the floor, with your legs slightly apart and your arms outstretched by your sides, palms up.

- Close your eyes and relax your breathing, letting go of any tension.

BEGINNER	ADVANCED
Hold Reclined Twists for 3 breaths. Perform Reclined Twists once on each side before performing Corpse Pose. Hold corpse pose for a few minutes.	Hold Reclined Twists for 5 breaths. Perform Reclined Twists 3 times on each side before performing Corpse Pose. Hold Corpse Pose for a few minutes.

#1 MOUNTAIN POSE TO REACH UP

(TADASANA TO URDHVA HASTASANA)

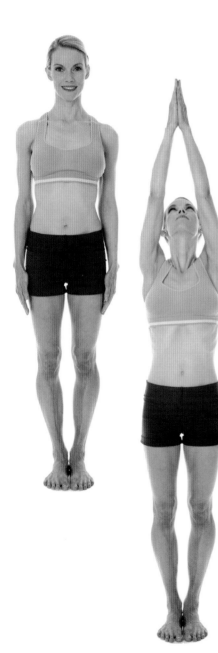

MOUNTAIN POSE

- Stand upright looking straight ahead, with your hands by your sides and your feet firmly planted on the mat.

- Lift your abdomen in and upward.

- Your weight should be balanced evenly on both feet.

REACH UP

- Raise your hands together above your head, and look straight up.

- Keep your shoulders from lifting and your ribs from jutting out.

- Hug your elbows toward the midline.

BEGINNER	ADVANCED
Hold each pose for 1 breath.	Hold each pose for 1 breath.

#2 STANDING FORWARD BEND
(UTTANASANA)

- Lower your arms back down by your sides.

- Inhale and bend forward from your hips, keeping your legs straight.

- Lower your torso down to rest your head on your shins, lengthening your spine.

- Place your hands flat on the floor beside your feet.

- If you cannot perform the pose with your legs straight, bend your knees slightly.

BEGINNER	ADVANCED
Hold the pose for 1 breath.	Hold the pose for 1 breath.

#3 LUNGE

(UTTHITA ASHWA SANCHALANASANA)

- Step one foot backward, completely straightening your leg.

- Press firmly through the heel, and keep your hips level.

- Place your hands on the floor to either side of your lead foot to establish balance.

- Maintain a neutral spine, looking straight ahead.

- Keep the knee of your lead foot directly over the ankle.

BEGINNER	ADVANCED
Hold the pose for 1 breath. Perform this pose once on each side.	Hold the pose for 1 breath. Perform this pose once on each side.

#4 PLANK

- Step your other foot back and lower your body toward the floor until your shoulders are directly over your hands, with your arms straight.

- Your body should be completely straight, from heels to head.

- Look down at the floor, keeping your head in line with your spine.

BEGINNER	ADVANCED
Hold the pose for 1 breath.	Hold the pose for 1 breath.

KNEES CHEST CHIN

- From Plank position, lower your knees to the floor, followed by your chest and your chin.

- Make sure your elbows bend straight back, not to the sides.

- Keep a slight arch in your lower back and hold your abdomen in.

BABY COBRA

- From the Knees Chest Chin pose, slide forward onto your belly and point your toes, with the tops of your feet on the mat.

- Pull your shoulders back, opening your chest, and gaze down the tip of your nose.

BEGINNER	ADVANCED
Hold each pose for 1 breath.	Hold each pose for 1 breath.

#6 DOWNWARD FACING DOG
(ADHO MUKHA SVANASANA)

- Push back with your hands and raise your hips high into the air to make a straight line from your hips to your hands.

- Straighten your legs and lengthen your heels toward the floor.

- Lengthen your spine and look toward your navel.

- Your hands should be in front of your shoulders, with your fingers spread.

BEGINNER	ADVANCED
Hold the pose for 1 breath.	Hold the pose for 1 breath.

#7 LUNGE

(UTTHITA ASHWA SANCHALANASANA)

- Step forward with one foot, bending your front knee.

- Press firmly through the heel, keeping your hips level.

- Place your hands on the floor to either side of your lead foot to establish balance.

- Maintain a neutral spine, looking straight ahead.

- Keep the knee of your lead foot directly over your ankle.

BEGINNER	ADVANCED
Hold the pose for 1 breath. Perform this pose once on each side.	Hold the pose for 1 breath. Perform this pose once on each side.

#8 STANDING FORWARD BEND

(UTTANASANA)

- Stand upright, bringing your feet together.

- Inhale and bend forward from the hips, keeping your legs straight.

- Lower your torso down to rest your head on your shins, lengthening your spine.

- Place your hands on the floor beside your feet.

- If you cannot perform the pose with your legs straight, bend your knees slightly.

BEGINNER	ADVANCED
Hold the pose for 1 breath.	Hold the pose for 1 breath.

#9 REACH UP TO MOUNTAIN POSE

(URDHVA HASTASANA TO TADASANA)

REACH UP

- Return to an upright position. Raise your hands together above your head, and look straight up.

- Keep your shoulders from lifting and your ribs from jutting out.

- Hug your elbows toward the midline.

MOUNTAIN POSE

- Lower your arms back by your sides, and look straight ahead, with your feet firmly planted on the mat.

- Lift your abdomen in and upward.

- Your weight should be balanced evenly on both feet.

BEGINNER	ADVANCED
Hold each pose for 1 breath.	Hold each pose for 1 breath.

LEVEL 2: FLOW 1

#10 HIGH LUNGE

- Step backward, straightening your back leg.

- Keep your torso upright while bending the knee of the front leg and pressing firmly through your heel, keeping your hips level.

- Raise your arms straight overhead, maintaining a neutral spine and looking straight ahead.

- Keep the knee of your lead foot directly over your ankle.

BEGINNER	ADVANCED
Hold the pose for 3 breaths. Perform this pose once on each side.	Hold the pose for 5 breaths. Perform this pose 3 times on each side.

#11 EAGLE POSE

(GARUDASANA)

- Step back to an upright position, slightly bend your knees, and lift your right foot to cross your right thigh over your left leg and hook your foot behind your lower calf.

- Wrap your right arm on top of your left, bending your elbows and raising your forearms straight up.

- The palms of your hands should be touching.

BEGINNER	ADVANCED
Hold the pose for 3 breaths. Perform this pose once on each side.	Hold the pose for 5 breaths. Perform this pose 3 times on each side.

#12 STANDING FORWARD BEND

(UTTANASANA)

- Stand upright, with your feet about hip-width apart.

- Inhale and bend forward from your hips, keeping your legs straight and your feet apart.

- Lower your torso down to rest your head on your shins, lengthening your spine.

- Hold your big toes or grab your ankles from behind with your elbows bent.

- If you cannot perform the pose with your legs straight, bend your knees slightly.

BEGINNER	ADVANCED
Hold the pose for 3 breaths.	Hold the pose for 5 breaths.

#13 EXTENDED HAND TO BIG TOE

(UTTHITA HASTA PADANGUSTHASANA)

- Return to an upright position, and lift one foot off the floor, bending at the knee.

- Take hold of your big toe with the same side hand, and slowly straighten your leg out in front of you.

- Press through your heel, and gently pull back on your toe.

- Rotate your leg out to the side.

BEGINNER	ADVANCED
Hold the pose for 3 breaths. Perform this pose once on each side.	Hold the pose for 5 breaths. Perform this pose once on each side.

#14 CROW POSE

(BAKASANA)

- Squat down and place your hands on the floor, with your upper arms against your shins.

- Squeeze your inner thighs high up on your arms as you lift your feet off the floor.

- Lean forward with your legs balanced on the backs of your upper arms, and straighten your arms as much as possible.

BEGINNER	ADVANCED
Hold the pose for 3 breaths.	Hold the pose for 5 breaths.

#15 SIDE CROW POSE

(PARSVA BAKASANA)

- Lower yourself from Crow Pose, turn your knees out to one side, and lean forward, placing your thigh on the back of your upper arm.

- Slowly take one foot off the floor at a time as you balance on the back of your upper arm.

- Keep your head up and look straight ahead.

BEGINNER	ADVANCED
Hold the pose for 3 breaths. Perform this pose once on each side.	Hold the pose for 5 breaths. Perform this pose once on each side.

#16 COBBLER'S POSE
(BADDHA KONASANA)

- Sit with your legs straight out in front of you.

- Bend your knees, and pull your heels toward your pelvis.

- Lower your knees out to the sides, and bring the soles of your feet together.

- Bend forward from the hips, and lower your head to your feet.

BEGINNER	ADVANCED
Hold the pose for 3 breaths.	Hold the pose for 5 breaths.

#17 BOAT POSE TO CANOE POSE

(NAVASANA TO URDHVA NAVASANA)

BOAT POSE

- Straighten your legs out in front again, and bring your arms by your sides.

- Bend your knees, and lift your feet off the floor.

- Lean back slightly as you raise and straighten your legs.

- Bring your arms up straight till they are parallel with the floor.

- Keep your chest up, and do not round your lower back. Stay long in the spine.

CANOE POSE

- From Boat, lean back toward the floor as you keep your arms and legs straight.

- Keep your chest up, and do not round your lower back. Stay long in the spine.

BEGINNER	ADVANCED
Hold each pose for 3 breaths.	Hold each pose for 5 breaths.

#18 SEATED ANGLE POSE
(UPAVISTHA KONASANA)

- Sit upright, with your legs straight out in front of you and your hands reaching to your toes.

- Slowly open your legs straight out to the sides.

- Keep your feet and knees pointing to the ceiling.

- Bend forward from your hips, and reach your hands toward your feet.

- Lengthen out from your lower back.

BEGINNER	ADVANCED
Hold the pose for 3 breaths.	Hold the pose for 5 breaths.

- Come upright, keeping your legs out to the sides, with feet and knees pointing to the ceiling.

- Raise one arm up over your head, and reach sideways to the opposite foot.

- Place your other arm on the floor in front.

- Lengthen out from your lower back.

BEGINNER	ADVANCED
Hold the pose for 3 breaths. Perform this pose once on each side.	Hold the pose for 5 breaths. Perform this pose 3 times on each side.

#20 INCLINED PLANE POSE

(PURVOTTANASANA)

- Sit upright, and bring your legs straight out in front of you.

- Place your hands about 12 inches behind your buttocks, palms down.

- Lift your hips off the floor, dropping your head back. Keep your legs straight and feet pointed.

- Come up to a straight-arm position, and let your head drop backward if you find that comfortable.

BEGINNER	ADVANCED
Hold the pose for 3 breaths.	Hold the pose for 5 breaths.

#21 FISH POSE

(MATSYASANA)

- Lower yourself back to the mat and lie on your back, with your legs straight out in front of you and your arms by your sides.

- Press your forearms into the mat, and gently arch your back, lifting your head and shoulders up off the floor.

- Drop the top of your head back to the mat, keeping your back arched and your shoulders raised.

BEGINNER	ADVANCED
Hold the pose for 3 breaths.	Hold the pose for 5 breaths.

#22 RECLINED TWISTS EAGLE LEGS

- Lie flat on your back again, with your legs extended straight out in front of you.

- Bring your knees into your chest, cross your left thigh over your right leg, and hook your foot behind the lower calf.

- Slowly lower your legs down to the side of the lower leg.

- Place your hand on your top knee to help ease your legs to the floor.

- Turn your head to the opposite side, and look toward the fingers of your outstretched arm.

BEGINNER	ADVANCED
Hold the pose for 3 breaths. Perform this pose once on each side.	Hold the pose for 5 breaths. Perform this pose 3 times on each side.

#23 EAGLE CRUNCHES TO CORPSE POSE

(EAGLE CRUNCHES TO SAVASANA)

EAGLE CRUNCHES

- Return to the mid-position, with your legs still in Eagle.

- Wrap your right arm on top of your left, bending your elbows and raising your forearms straight up. The palms of your hands should be touching.

- Perform a crunch, bringing your elbows to touch your knees in the middle.

CORPSE POSE

- Lie flat on your back on the floor, with your legs slightly apart and your arms out-stretched by your sides, palms up.

- Close your eyes and relax your breathing, letting go of any tension.

BEGINNER	ADVANCED
Perform 3 reps of crunches before going into Corpse Pose. Hold Corpse Pose for a few minutes.	Perform 5 reps of crunches before going into Corpse Pose. Hold Corpse Pose for a few minutes.

#13 FIERCE POSE

(UTKATASANA)

Perform the first twelve poses from Level 2, Flow 1 (pages 39–50), before moving on to these new poses.

- Raise your arms straight up overhead, bringing your palms together.

- Bend your hips and knees as if sitting into a chair.

- Keep your torso upright.

- Look up at your hands and lengthen your spine, opening your shoulders.

BEGINNER	ADVANCED
Hold the pose for 3 breaths.	Hold the pose for 5 breaths.

#14 STANDING FORWARD BEND

(UTTANASANA)

- Stand upright, lowering your arms.

- Bend forward from your hips, keeping your legs straight.

- Lower your torso down to rest your head on your shins, lengthening your spine.

- Place your hands flat on the floor beside your feet.

- If you cannot perform the pose with your legs straight, bend your knees slightly.

BEGINNER	ADVANCED
Hold the pose for 3 breaths.	Hold the pose for 5 breaths.

#15 PREPARE TO PLANK

(ARDHA UTTANASANA TO PLANK)

PREPARE

* Raise your head and shoulders to look forward, keeping your fingers touching the floor.

PLANK

* Place your hands back flat on the floor.

* Inhale and step back to Plank position, one foot at a time.

* Your body should be straight from heels to head, with your hands directly under your shoulders.

BEGINNER	ADVANCED
Hold each pose for 3 breaths.	Hold each pose for 5 breaths.

- From Plank position, lower your body closer to the floor by bending your elbows.

- Your body should be completely straight, from heels to head.

- Look slightly forward at the floor, keeping your head in line with your spine.

BEGINNER	ADVANCED
Hold the pose for 3 breaths.	Hold the pose for 5 breaths.

#17 UPWARD FACING DOG
(URDHVA MUKHA SVANASANA)

- From Chaturanga, press up through your hands and slide slightly forward, keeping your torso and thighs off the floor.

- Press the top of your feet into the floor.

- Look down along your nose, not up.

BEGINNER	ADVANCED
Hold the pose for 3 breaths.	Hold the pose for 5 breaths.

#18 DOWNWARD FACING DOG

(ADHO MUKHA SVANASANA)

- Push back with your hands, and raise your hips high into the air to form a straight line from your hips to your hands.

- Straighten your legs and lengthen your heels toward the floor.

- Lengthen your spine and look toward your navel.

- Your hands should be in front of your shoulders, with your fingers spread.

BEGINNER	ADVANCED
Hold the pose for 3 breaths.	Hold the pose for 5 breaths.

#19 WARRIOR I RIGHT

(VIRABHADRASANA I)

- Stand upright, and take one step back about 4 feet with your left leg, turning your left foot out slightly.

- Raise your arms straight overhead without lifting your shoulders, touching your palms together, and look up at your fingers.

- Bend your front knee so it is directly over your ankle.

- Make sure to ground your back heel into the mat, and at the same time try to keep your hips facing forward.

BEGINNER	ADVANCED
Hold the pose for 3 breaths. Perform this pose once on your right side.	Hold the pose for 5 breaths. Perform this pose 3 times on your right side.

- From a standing position, step back into a push-up position.

- Inhale and lower your body closer to the floor by bending your elbows.

- Your body should be completely straight, from your heels to your head.

- Look down at the floor, keeping your head in line with your spine.

BEGINNER	ADVANCED
Hold the pose for 3 breaths.	Hold the pose for 5 breaths.

#21 UPWARD FACING DOG

(URDHVA MUKHA SVANASANA)

- From Chaturanga, press up through your hands and slide slightly forward, keeping your torso and thighs off the floor.

- Press the tops of your feet into the floor.

- Look down along your nose, not up.

BEGINNER	ADVANCED
Hold the pose for 3 breaths.	Hold the pose for 5 breaths.

#22 DOWNWARD FACING DOG

(ADHO MUKHA SVANASANA)

- Push back with your hands, and raise your hips high into the air.

- Straighten your legs and lengthen your heels toward the floor.

- Lengthen your spine and look toward your navel.

- Your hands should be in front of your shoulders, with your fingers spread.

BEGINNER	ADVANCED
Hold the pose for 3 breaths.	Hold the pose for 5 breaths.

#23 WARRIOR I LEFT
(VIRABHADRASANA I)

- Stand upright, and take one step back about 4 feet on the right side, turning your right foot out slightly.

- Raise your arms straight overhead without lifting your shoulders, touching your palms together, and look up at your fingers.

- Bend your front knee so it is directly over your ankle.

- Make sure to ground your back heel into the mat, and at the same time try to keep your hips facing forward.

BEGINNER	ADVANCED
Hold the pose for 3 breaths. Perform this pose once on your left side.	Hold the pose for 5 breaths. Perform this pose 3 times on your left side.

- From a standing position, step back into a push-up position.

- Inhale and lower your body closer to the floor by bending your elbows.

- Your body should be completely straight from your heels to your head.

- Look down at the floor, keeping your head in line with your spine.

BEGINNER	ADVANCED
Hold the pose for 3 breaths.	Hold the pose for 5 breaths.

#25 UPWARD FACING DOG
(URDHVA MUKHA SVANASANA)

- From Chaturanga, press up through your hands and slide slightly forward, keeping your torso and thighs off the floor.

- Press the tops of your feet into the floor.

- Look down along your nose, not up.

BEGINNER	ADVANCED
Hold the pose for 3 breaths.	Hold the pose for 5 breaths.

#26 DOWNWARD FACING DOG

(ADHO MUKHA SVANASANA)

- Push back with your hands, and raise your hips high into the air to form a straight line from your hips to your hands.

- Straighten your legs and lengthen your heels toward the floor.

- Lengthen your spine and look toward your navel.

- Your hands should be in front of your shoulders, with your fingers spread.

BEGINNER	ADVANCED
Hold the pose for 3 breaths.	Hold the pose for 5 breaths.

#27 STANDING FORWARD BEND

(UTTANASANA)

- Step forward from Downward Facing Dog, walking your feet back to your hands.

- Fold from the hips into a forward bend, bringing your head to rest on your knees.

BEGINNER	ADVANCED
Hold the pose for 3 breaths.	Hold the pose for 5 breaths.

#28 FIERCE POSE

(UTKATASANA)

- Raise your arms straight up overhead, bringing your palms together.

- Bend your hips and knees as if you were sitting in a chair.

- Keep your torso upright.

- Look up at your hands and lengthen your spine, opening your shoulders.

BEGINNER	ADVANCED
Hold the pose for 3 breaths.	Hold the pose for 5 breaths.

#29 MOUNTAIN POSE
(TADASANA)

- Stand upright looking straight ahead, with your hands by your sides and your feet firmly planted on the mat.

- Lift your abdomen in and upward.

- Your weight should be balanced evenly on both feet.

BEGINNER	ADVANCED
Hold the pose for 3 breaths.	Hold the pose for 5 breaths.

#30 WARRIOR SEQUENCE

(VIRABHADRASANA SEQUENCE)

WARRIOR I

- Stand back upright, and step one leg back about 4 feet, turning your back foot out slightly.

- Raise your arms straight overhead, touching your palms together, and look up at your fingers.

- Bend your front knee so it is directly over your ankle. Keep your hips facing forward.

WARRIOR II

- Lower your arms until they are parallel to the floor, palms down, and reach out to both sides.

- Open your torso to the side. Turn your head to look forward along your arm.

WARRIOR III

- Step forward to an upright position. Lengthen your torso to bend forward until your torso is parallel to the floor.

- Lift your back leg up behind you, bringing your arms up by your sides, to also be parallel to the floor.

- Keep your hips level, and lift your ribs, stretching the raised leg back behind you.

- Your head and neck should be straight and in line with your torso.

BEGINNER	ADVANCED
Hold each pose for 3 breaths. Perform this sequence once on each side.	Hold each pose for 5 breaths. Perform this sequence 3 times on each side.

#31 HALF MOON POSE
(ARDHA CHANDRASANA)

- Open through the chest, and twist your torso and one arm to look up at the ceiling.

- Turn your back leg out 90 degrees so your toes are pointing straight out to the side.

- Lower the other hand down to touch the floor.

BEGINNER	ADVANCED
Hold the pose for 3 breaths. Perform this pose once on each side.	Hold the pose for 5 breaths. Perform this pose 3 times on each side.

(VRKSASANA)

- Return to stand upright, and raise one leg, bending at the knee and placing the sole of your foot on the inside of your opposite thigh.

- Raise your arm over your head, reaching over to the other side and bending your torso slightly.

- Rest your other hand on your thigh.

- Stay grounded through the entire foot of the standing leg.

BEGINNER	ADVANCED
Hold the pose for 3 breaths. Perform this pose once on each side.	Hold the pose for 5 breaths. Perform this pose 3 times on each side.

#33 TRIANGLE POSE TO EXTENDED ANGLE

(TRIKONASANA TO PARSVOTTANASANA)

TRIANGLE POSE

- Return to an upright position, with your arms by your sides.

- Step apart one leg-length, turning your front foot out 90 degrees to the side and your back foot inward 75 degrees.

- Lower your hand to the floor behind your front foot, and stretch your other hand toward the ceiling, keeping it in line with the hand on the floor.

- Make sure to lengthen through both sides of your waist.

EXTENDED ANGLE

- From the Triangle Pose, bend your front knee and rest your elbow on it.

- Stretch your other arm above your head as you extend the lower arm over to the side of the front foot.

- Look up to the ceiling, keeping your shoulders relaxed.

- Try to form a straight line from the back foot out to the tops of the fingers above.

BEGINNER	ADVANCED
Hold each pose for 3 breaths. Perform this sequence once on each side.	Hold each pose for 5 breaths. Perform this sequence 3 times on each side.

#34 WIDE LEG FORWARD BEND WITH TOE LOCK

(PRASARITA PADOTTANASANA)

BEGINNER	ADVANCED
Hold the pose for 3 breaths.	Hold the pose for 5 breaths.

- Return to an upright position, with your feet still spread.

- Place your hands on your hips, and press firmly through the outer edges of your feet, lifting your inner arches.

- Exhale and bend forward at your hips.

- Lower your head and hands to the mat, placing your hands below your shoulders, with your elbows bent behind you. Grip your big toes.

- Stand upright, and step to the front of the mat.

#35 SIDEWAYS INTENSE STRETCH

(PARSVOTTANASANA)

- Stand upright, and step one leg back about 4 feet.

- Bend forward from the hips, bringing your head down to the front knee, lengthening through the spine.

- Place your hands on the floor to the sides of the front foot.

- Keep both legs straight and your feet flat.

BEGINNER	ADVANCED
Hold the pose for 3 breaths.	Hold the pose for 5 breaths.

#36 REVOLVED TRIANGLE

(PARIVRTTA TRIKONASANA)

- Raise the arm on the same side as the front foot, stretching your hand toward the ceiling.

- Place the other hand on the outside of the front foot, keeping it in line with your top hand.

- Twist from your waist, not your hips.

- Your head should turn away from your tailbone.

BEGINNER	ADVANCED
Hold the pose for 3 breaths. Perform this pose once on each side.	Hold the pose for 5 breaths. Perform this pose 3 times on each side.

#37 SEATED FORWARD BEND

(PASCHIMOTTANASANA)

- Sit on the floor, holding your big toes, with your legs straight out in front of you.

- Bend forward at the hips, and lower your head toward your knees.

- Reach your hands past your feet, and clasp them together if possible.

- Do not tuck your tailbone under; stay centered on your sit bones.

- Lengthen your spine, and keep your feet flexed.

BEGINNER	ADVANCED
Hold the pose for 3 breaths.	Hold the pose for 5 breaths.

#38 HEAD TO KNEE

(PARIVRTTA JANU SIRSASANA)

- Sit back upright, bend one knee, and place the sole of your foot into the opposite inner thigh.

- Bend forward at the hips, and lower your head toward your straight knee.

- Reach your hands to your out-stretched foot, clasping it if possible.

- Stay centered on your sit bones.

- Lengthen your spine, and keep your foot flexed.

BEGINNER	ADVANCED
Hold the pose for 3 breaths. Perform this pose once on each side.	Hold the pose for 5 breaths. Perform this pose 3 times on each side.

#39 SIDE STRETCH HEAD TO KNEE

(PARIGHASANA)

- Sit upright, keeping the foot and knee of the straight leg pointing to the ceiling and the other foot in against your thigh.

- Raise the arm on the same side as the bent knee up over your head, and reach sideways to the opposite foot.

- Place your other arm on the floor in front of your straight leg.

- Lengthen out from your lower back.

BEGINNER	ADVANCED
Hold the pose for 3 breaths. Perform this pose once on each side.	Hold the pose for 5 breaths. Perform this pose 3 times on each side.

#40 HALF BRIDGE TO FULL BRIDGE

(SETU BANDHASANA)

HALF BRIDGE

- Lie flat on your back, with your knees bent and your feet flat on the mat and slightly apart, your arms by your sides.

- Inhale and lift your hips off the floor, rolling up onto your shoulders into a back bend.

- Bring your arms straight under your torso, clasping your hands together between your feet.

FULL BRIDGE

- From Half Bridge, place your hands flat on the floor to the sides of your head, with the fingers pointing toward your feet.

- Exhale and press your hands into the floor, lifting your hips, shoulders, and head.

- Straighten your arms, and drop your head to look toward the floor.

BEGINNER	ADVANCED
Hold each pose for 3 breaths.	Hold each pose for 5 breaths.

#41 SHOULDER STAND

(SARVANGASANA)

- From Full Bridge, lower yourself back to the floor to lie flat.

- Bring your knees to your chest, and lift your feet overhead, as if going into Plow pose.

- Press your arms into the floor. Bend your elbows, placing your hands on your lower back to support your body.

- Straighten your legs overhead, lifting your torso off the floor and bringing your hips directly over your shoulders.

BEGINNER	ADVANCED
Hold the pose for 3 breaths.	Hold the pose for 5 breaths.

(RECLINED TWISTS TO SAVASANA)

RECLINED TWISTS

- Lower from Shoulder Stand to lie on your back, with your legs extended straight and your arms stretched out to the sides.

- Bring one leg up straight, and then slowly lower it down to the opposite side while keeping the other leg straight.

- Use your hand to clasp your ankle or calf to help ease the leg to the floor.

- Turn your head to the opposite side, and look toward the fingers of your outstretched arm.

CORPSE POSE

- Lie flat on your back on the floor, with your legs slightly apart and your arms stretched out to your sides, palms up.

- Close your eyes and relax your breathing, letting go of any tension.

BEGINNER	ADVANCED
Hold Reclined Twists for 3 breaths. Perform Reclined Twists once on each side before going into Corpse Pose. Hold Corpse Pose for a few minutes.	Hold Reclined Twists for 5 breaths. Perform Reclined Twists 3 times on each side before going into Corpse Pose. Hold Corpse Pose for a few minutes.

#1 MOUNTAIN POSE TO REACH UP

(TADASANA TO URDHVA HASTASANA)

MOUNTAIN POSE
- Stand upright, looking straight ahead, with your hands by your sides and your feet firmly planted on the mat.

- Lift your abdomen in and upward.

- Your weight should be balanced evenly on both feet.

REACH UP
- Raise your hands together above your head, and look straight up.

- Keep your shoulders from lifting and your ribs from jutting out.

- Hug your elbows toward your midline.

BEGINNER	ADVANCED
Hold each pose for 1 breath.	Hold each pose for 1 breath.

#2 STANDING FORWARD BEND

(UTTANASANA)

- Lower your arms back by your sides.

- Bend forward from your hips, keeping your legs straight.

- Lower your torso down to rest your head on your shins, lengthening your spine.

- Place your hands flat on the floor beside your feet.

- If you cannot perform the pose with your legs straight, bend your knees slightly.

BEGINNER	ADVANCED
Hold the pose for 1 breath.	Hold the pose for 1 breath.

#3 PREPARE TO CHATURANGA

(ARDHA UTTANASANA TO CHATURANGA)

PREPARE

- Raise your head and shoulders to look forward, keeping only your fingers touching the floor.

CHATURANGA

- Place your hands flat on the floor.

- Inhale and step back one foot at a time to a Plank position.

- Exhale and lower your body closer to the floor, bending your elbows.

- Your body should be completely straight, from heels to head.

- Look down at the floor to keep your head in line with your spine.

BEGINNER	ADVANCED
Hold each pose for 1 breath.	Hold each pose for 1 breath.

#4 UPWARD FACING DOG

(URDHVA MUKHA SVANASANA)

- From Chaturanga, press up through your hands and slide slightly forward, keeping your torso and thighs off the floor.

- Press the tops of your feet into the floor.

- Look down along your nose, not up.

BEGINNER	ADVANCED
Hold the pose for 1 breath.	Hold the pose for 1 breath.

#5 DOWNWARD FACING DOG
(ADHO MUKHA SVANASANA)

- Push back with your hands, and raise your hips high into the air.

- Straighten your legs, and lengthen your heels toward the floor.

- Lengthen your spine, and look toward your navel.

- Your hands should be in front of your shoulders, with your fingers spread.

BEGINNER	ADVANCED
Hold the pose for 1 breath.	Hold the pose for 1 breath.

- Jump forward with both feet, keeping your hands flat on the mat.

- Land with both feet by your hands.

- Raise your head and shoulders to look forward, keeping your fingers touching the mat.

BEGINNER	ADVANCED
Hold the pose for 1 breath.	Hold the pose for 1 breath.

#7 STANDING FORWARD BEND
(UTTANASANA)

- Bend forward from your hips, keeping your legs straight.

- Lower your torso down to rest your head on your shins, lengthening your spine.

- Place your hands flat on the floor beside your feet.

- If you cannot perform the pose with your legs straight, bend your knees slightly.

BEGINNER	ADVANCED
Hold the pose for 1 breath.	Hold the pose for 1 breath.

#8 REACH UP TO MOUNTAIN POSE

(URDHVA HASTASANA TO TADASANA)

REACH UP

- Return to an upright position, raise your hands together above your head, and look straight up.

- Keep your shoulders from lifting and your ribs from jutting out.

- Hug your elbows toward your mid-line.

MOUNTAIN POSE

- Lower your arms back by your sides and look straight ahead, with your feet firmly planted.

- Lift your abdomen in and upward.

- Your weight should be balanced evenly on both feet.

BEGINNER	ADVANCED
Hold each pose for 1 breath.	Hold each pose for 1 breath.

#9 FIERCE POSE

(UTKATASANA)

- Raise your arms straight up over-head, bringing your palms together.

- Bend your hips and knees as if sitting in a chair.

- Keep your torso upright.

- Look up at your hands and lengthen your spine, opening your shoulders.

BEGINNER	ADVANCED
Hold the pose for 3 breaths.	Hold the pose for 5 breaths.

(PARIVRTTA UTKATASANA)

- From Fierce pose, lower your hands down in front of your chest, bending your elbows.

- Squat slightly deeper, and twist your torso to one side, bringing your elbow to the outside of your opposite knee.

- Look up toward the ceiling.

BEGINNER	ADVANCED
Hold the pose for 3 breaths. Perform this pose once on each side.	Hold the pose for 5 breaths. Perform this pose 3 times on each side.

#11 HIGH LUNGE

- Stand upright, and step one leg backward, straightening the leg.

- Keep your torso upright while bending the knee of the front leg and pressing firmly through the heel, keeping your hips level.

- Raise your arms straight overhead, maintaining a neutral spine and looking straight forward.

- Keep the knee of your lead foot directly over your ankle.

BEGINNER	ADVANCED
Hold the pose for 3 breaths. Perform this pose once on each side.	Hold the pose for 5 breaths. Perform this pose 3 times on each side.

#12 REVOLVED HALF MOON POSE

(PARIVRTTA ARDHA CHANDRASANA)

- Reach forward, raising your back leg straight up behind you.

- Bend forward at your hips, placing the hand on the same side as your raised leg down on the mat in front of the opposite foot.

- Raise the other arm straight up to the ceiling.

- Stack your hips one on top of the other, and open through your chest as you look up at your top hand.

BEGINNER	ADVANCED
Hold the pose for 3 breaths. Perform this pose once on each side.	Hold the pose for 5 breaths. Perform this pose 3 times on each side.

#13 EAGLE POSE

(GARUDASANA)

- Return to an upright position.

- Slightly bend your knees and lift your right leg, crossing your right thigh over your left leg and hooking your foot behind the lower calf.

- Wrap your right arm on top of your left, bending your elbows and raising your forearms straight up.

- Try to touch the palms of your hands together.

BEGINNER	ADVANCED
Hold the pose for 3 breaths. Perform this pose once on each side.	Hold the pose for 5 breaths. Perform this pose 3 times on each side.

#14 DANCING SHIVA

(NATARAJASANA)

LEVEL 3: FLOW 1

- Release from Eagle, and stand upright with your arms by your sides.

- Raise one leg up behind you, bending at the knee while keeping your standing leg straight.

- Reach back with one hand to grab the foot of your raised leg, and gently pull it higher while raising the other hand up in front.

- Reach your other arm back to also hold the raised foot, and gently pull the foot toward the back of your head, arching back slightly.

BEGINNER	ADVANCED
Hold the pose for 3 breaths. Perform this pose once on each side.	Hold the pose for 5 breaths. Perform this pose 3 times on each side.

#15 STANDING FORWARD BEND

(UTTANASANA)

- Lower your leg back to the mat and step your feet slightly apart.

- Inhale and bend forward from your hips, keeping your legs straight.

- Lower your torso down to rest your head on your shins, lengthening your spine.

- Place your hands under your feet.

- If you cannot perform the pose with your legs straight, bend your knees slightly.

BEGINNER	ADVANCED
Hold the pose for 3 breaths.	Hold the pose for 5 breaths.

(UTTHITA HASTA PADANGUSTHASANA)

BEGINNER	ADVANCED
Hold the pose for 3 breaths. Perform this pose once on each side.	Hold the pose for 5 breaths. Perform this pose 3 times on each side.

- Come upright again, and lift one foot off the floor, bending at the knee.

- Take hold of your big toe with the hand on that same side, and slowly straighten your leg out in front.

- Press through your heel, and gently pull back on your toe.

- Rotate the leg out to the side.

#17 CROW POSE

(BAKASANA)

- Squat down, placing your hands on the mat with your upper arms against your shins.

- Squeeze your inner thighs high up on your arms as you lift your feet off the floor.

- Lean forward with your legs balanced on the backs of your upper arms, and straighten your arms as much as possible.

BEGINNER	ADVANCED
Hold the pose for 3 breaths.	Hold the pose for 5 breaths.

#18 SIDE CROW POSE

(PARSVA BAKASANA)

- Lower from Crow Pose, and turn your knees out to one side. Lean forward, placing your thigh on the back of your upper arm.

- Slowly take one foot off the floor at a time as you balance on the back of your upper arm.

- Keep your head up, and look straight ahead.

BEGINNER	ADVANCED
Hold the pose for 3 breaths. Perform this pose once on each side.	Hold the pose for 5 breaths. Perform this pose 3 times on each side.

#19 KING PIGEON POSE

(EKA PADA RAJAKAPOTASANA)

- Lower from Side Crow and straighten one leg back behind you.

- Slide your other leg across in front of you, bending your knee, with your shin parallel to the front of the mat.

- Bend forward at your hips, lowering your torso to the mat and resting your head on your hands folded in front of you.

- Keep your hips square, and let your stomach rest on your bent leg.

BEGINNER	ADVANCED
Hold the pose for 3 breaths. Perform this pose once on each side.	Hold the pose for 5 breaths. Perform this pose 3 times on each side.

#20 LOCUST POSE

(SHALABHASANA)

- Straighten both legs behind you, and lie facedown on the floor, with your arms by your sides.

- Raise your arms straight up behind your back, clasping your hands together.

- Raise your head and straight legs together up off the floor, resting on your stomach and upper thighs.

BEGINNER	ADVANCED
Hold the pose for 3 breaths.	Hold the pose for 5 breaths.

#21 BOW POSE
(DHANURASANA)

- From Locust, raise your arms straight up behind you, at the same time raising your head and legs together up off the floor, resting on your stomach and upper thighs.

- Bend at the knees and grab your ankles, gently pulling your feet toward your buttocks.

BEGINNER	ADVANCED
Hold the pose for 3 breaths.	Hold the pose for 5 breaths.

(BALASANA)

- Release from Bow Pose and go down to all fours, setting your hips onto the backs of your legs.

- Lower your torso onto your upper thighs and your head to the floor. Bring your arms straight by your sides with palms up.

BEGINNER	ADVANCED
Hold the pose for 3 breaths.	Hold the pose for 5 breaths.

#23 HEADSTAND
(SIRSASANA)

- Place your forearms on the floor with your hands clasped.

- Lower the top of your head between your forearms.

- Raise your hips, and walk your feet in toward your head until your legs are straight.

- Bend your knees into your armpits, and then straighten your legs.

- Keep your weight evenly balanced on your forearms.

BEGINNER	ADVANCED
Hold the pose for 3 breaths.	Hold the pose for 5 breaths.

#24 COBBLER'S POSE

(BADDHA KONASANA)

- Lower from Headstand to sit with your legs extended straight out in front of you.

- Bend your knees, and pull your heels in toward your pelvis.

- Lower your knees out to the sides, and bring the soles of your feet together.

- Bend forward from your hips, and lower your head to your feet.

BEGINNER	ADVANCED
Hold the pose for 3 breaths.	Hold the pose for 5 breaths.

#25 BOAT POSE TO CANOE POSE

(NAVASANA TO URDHVA NAVASANA)

BOAT POSE

- Sit upright with your legs extended straight out in front of you and your arms by your sides.

- Bend your knees, and lift your feet off the mat.

- Lean back slightly as you raise and straighten your legs.

- Bring your arms up straight until they are parallel with the floor.

- Keep your chest up, and do not round your lower back. Stay long in the spine.

CANOE POSE

- From Boat, lean back toward the floor, keeping your arms and legs straight.

- Keep your chest up, and do not round your lower back. Stay long in the spine.

BEGINNER	ADVANCED
Hold each pose for 3 breaths.	Hold each pose for 5 breaths.

#26 SEATED ANGLE POSE

(UPAVISTHA KONASANA)

- Sit upright with your legs extended straight out in front of you.

- Slowly open your legs straight out to the sides. Keep your feet and knees pointing to the ceiling.

- Bend forward from your hips and reach your hands toward your feet to grab your big toes.

- Lengthen out from your lower back.

BEGINNER	ADVANCED
Hold the pose for 3 breaths.	Hold the pose for 5 breaths.

#27 SEATED ANGLE WITH SIDE BENDS

- Come upright, keeping your legs out to the sides, with your feet and your knees pointing to the ceiling.

- Raise one arm up over your head, and reach sideways to the opposite foot.

- Place your other arm on the mat in front of you.

- Lengthen out from your lower back.

BEGINNER	ADVANCED
Hold the pose for 3 breaths. Perform this pose once on each side.	Hold the pose for 5 breaths. Perform this pose 3 times on each side.

- Sit upright in straddle, keeping your feet and knees pointing to the ceiling.

- Bend forward from your hips, and reach your hands to grab your big toes, pulling your knees into your chest.

- Lean back, and raise both legs straight up in the air to approximately shoulder height.

BEGINNER	ADVANCED
Hold the pose for 3 breaths.	Hold the pose for 5 breaths.

#29 WIDE ANGLE POSE
(SUPTA KONASANA)

- From Seated Angle with Legs Raised, roll back onto your shoulders, touching your feet to the floor behind your head.

BEGINNER	ADVANCED
Hold the pose for 3 breaths.	Hold the pose for 5 breaths.

#30 INCLINED PLANE POSE

(PURVOTTANASANA)

- Rock yourself back upright, bringing your legs straight out in front of you.

- Place your hands about 12 inches behind your buttocks, with your palms down.

- Inhale, lifting your hips off the floor and dropping your head back.

- Keep your legs straight and feet pointed.

- Come up to a straight-arm position, and let your head drop backward if you find that comfortable.

BEGINNER	ADVANCED
Hold the pose for 3 breaths.	Hold the pose for 5 breaths.

#31 FISH POSE WITH LEGS RAISED

(MATSYASANA)

- Lower your body back to the mat, and while pressing your forearms into the floor, gently arch your back, lifting your head and shoulders off the mat.

- Lower the top of your head back to the floor, keeping your back arched and your shoulders raised off the mat.

- Bring your arms and legs straight up in front, with your hands together.

BEGINNER	ADVANCED
Hold the pose for 3 breaths.	Hold the pose for 5 breaths.

BEGINNER	ADVANCED
Hold the pose for 3 breaths. Perform this pose once on each side.	Hold the pose for 5 breaths. Perform this pose 3 times on each side.

- Lie on your back with your knees bent, your feet flat, and your arms stretched out to the sides.

- Bring your knees into your chest, cross your left thigh over your right leg, and hook your foot behind the lower calf.

- Slowly lower your legs down to the right side.

- Place your right hand on your top knee to help ease the legs to the floor.

- Turn your head to the opposite side, and look toward the fingers of your outstretched arm.

#33 EAGLE CRUNCHES

- Return to the center position and wrap your right arm on top of your left, bending your elbows and raising your forearms straight up.

- The palms of your hands should be touching.

- Perform a crunch, bringing your elbows to touch your knees in the middle.

BEGINNER	ADVANCED
Perform 3 reps.	Perform 5 reps.

BEGINNER	ADVANCED
Perform 3 reps.	Perform 5 reps.

- Release from Eagle pose, and lie flat on your back with your legs straight up, your ankles directly over your hips, and your arms by your sides.

- Slowly lower your legs, stopping about 12 inches from the floor.

- Return to the top position.

#35 CORPSE POSE
(SAVASANA)

- Lie flat on your back on the mat, with your legs slightly apart and your arms outstretched by your sides, palms up.

- Close your eyes and relax your breathing, letting go of any tension.

BEGINNER	ADVANCED
Hold the pose for a few minutes.	Hold the pose for a few minutes.

#9 FIERCE POSE

(UTKATASANA)

Perform the first eight poses from Level 3, Flow 1 (pages 92–99), before moving on to these new poses.

- Raise your arms straight up overhead, bringing your palms together.

- Bend your hips and knees as if sitting into a chair.

- Keep your torso upright.

- Look up at your hands and lengthen your spine, opening your shoulders.

BEGINNER	ADVANCED
Hold the pose for 3 breaths.	Hold the pose for 5 breaths.

#10 STANDING FORWARD BEND
(UTTANASANA)

- Stand upright with your feet together.

- Inhale and bend forward from your hips, keeping your legs straight.

- Lower your torso down to rest your head on your shins, lengthening your spine.

- Place your hands flat on the floor beside your feet.

- If you cannot perform the pose with your legs straight, bend your knees slightly.

BEGINNER	ADVANCED
Hold the pose for 3 breaths.	Hold the pose for 5 breaths.

#11 PREPARE TO CHATURANGA

(ARDHA UTTANASANA TO CHATURANGA)

PREPARE
- Raise your head and shoulders to look forward, keeping only your fingers touching the mat.

CHATURANGA
- Jump back, lowering your body down into Plank position.

- Drop even closer toward the floor, bending your elbows.

- Your body should be completely straight from heels to head.

- Look down at the floor, keeping your head in line with your spine.

BEGINNER	ADVANCED
Hold each pose for 3 breaths.	Hold each pose for 5 breaths.

#12 UPWARD FACING DOG

(URDHVA MUKHA SVANASANA)

- From Chaturanga, press up through your hands and slide slightly forward, keeping your torso and thighs off the mat.

- Press the tops of your feet into the mat.

- Look down along your nose, not up.

BEGINNER	ADVANCED
Hold the pose for 3 breaths.	Hold the pose for 5 breaths.

(ADHO MUKHA SVANASANA)

- Push back with your hands and raise your hips high into the air.

- Straighten your legs, and lengthen your heels toward the floor.

- Lengthen your spine, and look toward your navel.

- Your hands should be in front of your shoulders, with your fingers spread apart.

BEGINNER	ADVANCED
Hold the pose for 3 breaths.	Hold the pose for 5 breaths.

#14 WARRIOR SEQUENCE RIGHT

(VIRABHADRASANA SEQUENCE)

WARRIOR I RIGHT

- Step your left leg back about 4 feet, and turn the foot out slightly.

- Raise your arms straight overhead without lifting your shoulders, touching your palms together, and look up at your fingers.

- Bend your front knee so it is directly over your ankle.

- Make sure to ground your back heel into the floor, and at the same time try to keep your hips facing forward.

WARRIOR II RIGHT

- Lower your arms, palms down, until they are parallel to the floor, and reach out to both sides.

- Open your torso to the side.

- Turn your head to look forward along your arm to the tips of your fingers.

BEGINNER	ADVANCED
Hold each pose for 3 breaths. Perform this sequence once on your right side.	Hold each pose for 5 breaths. Perform this sequence 3 times on your right side.

- Step back, and drop your body into Plank position.

- Further lower yourself toward the mat, bending your elbows.

- Your body should be completely straight from heels to head.

- Look down at the floor, keeping your head in line with your spine.

BEGINNER	ADVANCED
Hold the pose for 3 breaths.	Hold the pose for 5 breaths.

#16 UPWARD FACING DOG

(URDHVA MUKHA SVANASANA)

- From Chaturanga, press up through your hands and slide slightly forward, keeping your torso and thighs off the mat.

- Press the tops of your feet into the mat.

- Look down along your nose, not up.

BEGINNER	ADVANCED
Hold the pose for 3 breaths.	Hold the pose for 5 breaths.

#17 DOWNWARD FACING DOG

(ADHO MUKHA SVANASANA)

- Push back with your hands, and raise your hips high into the air.

- Straighten your legs and lengthen your heels toward the floor.

- Lengthen your spine, and look toward your navel.

- Your hands should be in front of your shoulders, with your fingers spread apart.

BEGINNER	ADVANCED
Hold the pose for 3 breaths.	Hold the pose for 5 breaths.

#18 WARRIOR SEQUENCE LEFT

(VIRABHADRASANA SEQUENCE)

WARRIOR I LEFT

- Stand upright and step your right leg back about 4 feet, turning your foot out slightly.

- Without lifting your shoulders, raise your arms straight overhead, touching your palms together and looking up at your fingers.

- Make sure to ground your back heel into the mat, and at the same time try to keep your hips facing forward.

WARRIOR II LEFT

- Lower your arms with your palms down until they are parallel to the floor, and reach out to both sides.

- Open your torso to the side.

- Turn your head to look forward along your arm to the tips of your fingers.

BEGINNER	ADVANCED
Hold each pose for 3 breaths. Perform this sequence once on your left side.	Hold each pose for 5 breaths. Perform this sequence 3 times on your left side.

- Step back, dropping your body into Plank position.

- Further lower yourself toward the floor, bending at the elbows.

- Your body should be completely straight, from heels to head.

- Look down at the floor, keeping your head in line with your spine.

BEGINNER	ADVANCED
Hold the pose for 3 breaths.	Hold the pose for 5 breaths.

#20 UPWARD FACING DOG

(URDHVA MUKHA SVANASANA)

- From Chaturanga, press up through your hands and slide slightly forward, keeping your torso and thighs off the mat.

- Press the tops of your feet into the mat.

- Look down along your nose, not up.

BEGINNER	ADVANCED
Hold the pose for 3 breaths.	Hold the pose for 5 breaths.

(ADHO MUKHA SVANASANA)

- Push back with your hands, and raise your hips high into the air.

- Straighten your legs and lengthen your heels toward the floor.

- Lengthen your spine and look toward your navel.

- Your hands should be in front of your shoulders, with your fingers spread apart.

BEGINNER	ADVANCED
Hold the pose for 3 breaths.	Hold the pose for 5 breaths.

#22 JUMP FORWARD

- Jump forward with both feet, keeping your hands flat on the mat.

- Land with both feet by your hands.

- Raise your head and shoulders to look forward, keeping your fingers touching the mat.

BEGINNER	ADVANCED
Hold the pose for 3 breaths.	Hold the pose for 5 breaths.

#23 WARRIOR I VARIATION

(VIRABHADRASANA I)

- Step one leg back about 4 feet, turning the foot out slightly.

- With your arms straight, clasp your hands together behind your back, and lean backward, looking slightly toward the ceiling.

- Make sure to ground your back heel into the mat, and at the same time, try to keep your hips facing forward.

- Bend forward at your hips, lowering your head inside your front knee and bringing your clasped hands forward.

BEGINNER	ADVANCED
Hold the pose for 3 breaths. Perform this pose once on each side.	Hold the pose for 5 breaths. Perform this pose 3 times on each side.

#24 WARRIOR II

(VIRABHADRASANA II)

- Return upright, and lower your arms with your palms down until they are parallel to the floor, and reach out to both sides.

- Open your torso to the side.

- Turn your head to look forward along your arm to the tips of your fingers.

BEGINNER	ADVANCED
Hold the pose for 3 breaths. Perform this pose once on each side.	Hold the pose for 5 breaths. Perform this pose 3 times on each side.

(VIRABHADRASANA III)

- Step forward to an upright position.

- Lift your back leg up behind you until it is parallel to the floor and bring your arms up by your sides, also parallel to the floor.

- Keep your hips level and lift your ribs, stretching the raised leg back behind you.

- Your head and neck should be straight and in line with your torso.

BEGINNER	ADVANCED
Hold the pose for 3 breaths. Perform this pose once on each side.	Hold the pose for 5 breaths. Perform this pose 3 times on each side.

#26 HALF MOON POSE WITH LEG BEND

(ADVANCED ARDHA CHANDRASANA)

- From Warrior III, place your same-side hand down on the floor in front of the standing foot.

- Bend your raised leg, catching your foot and pulling it toward your buttocks.

- Stack your hips one on top of the other, and open through the chest as you look up at the ceiling.

BEGINNER	ADVANCED
Hold the pose for 3 breaths. Perform this pose once on each side.	Hold the pose for 5 breaths. Perform this pose 3 times on each side.

#27 STANDING SPLIT POSE

(URDHVA PRASARITA EKA PADASANA)

- Release your foot, and raise the back leg high.

- Place your hands on the floor, to the sides of your standing foot.

- Lower your head toward the knee of your standing leg.

- Raise your arms straight up behind your back, clasping your hands together.

BEGINNER	ADVANCED
Hold the pose for 3 breaths. Perform this pose once on each side.	Hold the pose for 5 breaths. Perform this pose 3 times on each side.

#28 STANDING BOUND HALF LOTUS POSE

(ARDHA BADDHA PASCHIMOTTANASANA)

- Stand upright with your arms by your sides.

- Raise one foot, bending at the knee and holding the shin. Pull the foot up to your hip.

- Reach behind your back with the arm on the same side as your raised foot to grasp it.

- Raise your other arm straight up overhead.

- Bend forward at your hips, lowering your head to the knee of your standing leg.

- Place your hand on the floor beside your standing foot while still holding the other foot by your hip.

BEGINNER	ADVANCED
Hold the pose for 3 breaths. Perform this pose once on each side.	Hold the pose for 5 breaths. Perform this pose 3 times on each side.

#29 TRIANGLE POSE TO EXTENDED ANGLE WITH BEND

(TRIKONASANA TO PARSVOTTANASANA)

TRIANGLE POSE

- Return to an upright position with your arms by your sides.

- Step apart a few feet, turning your front foot out 90 degrees to the side.

- Lower your same-side hand to the floor behind your front foot, and stretch your other hand toward the ceiling, keeping it in line with the hand on the floor.

EXTENDED ANGLE WITH BEND

- From Triangle Pose, bend your front knee and rest your elbow on the knee of this leg.

- Lower the other arm, wrapping it behind your back and clasping your hands under the thigh of your bent leg.

- Look up to the ceiling, keeping your shoulders relaxed.

- Try to form a straight line from the back foot out to your shoulder.

BEGINNER	ADVANCED
Hold each pose for 3 breaths. Perform this sequence once on each side.	Hold each pose for 5 breaths. Perform this sequence 3 times on each side.

#30 WIDE LEG FORWARD BEND WITH CLASP

(PRASARITA PADOTTANASANA)

- From an upright position, spread your legs about 4 feet wide.

- Bring your arms straight behind your back, clasping your hands together.

- Press firmly through the outer edges of your feet, lifting your inner arches.

- Bend forward at your hips, lowering your head to the floor and bringing your clasped hands forward.

BEGINNER	ADVANCED
Hold the pose for 3 breaths.	Hold the pose for 5 breaths.

#31 SIDEWAYS INTENSE STRETCH

(PARSVOTTANASANA)

- Stand upright, and step one leg back about 4 feet.

- Bend forward from your hips, bringing your head down to your front knee and lengthening through your spine.

- Bring your palms together behind your back with your fingers pointing toward your head.

- Keep both legs straight and your feet flat.

BEGINNER	ADVANCED
Hold the pose for 3 breaths. Perform this pose once on each side.	Hold the pose for 5 breaths. Perform this pose 3 times on each side.

#32 REVOLVED TRIANGLE

(PARIVRTTA TRIKONASANA)

- Turn your back foot out slightly.

- Bring your arms up until they are parallel to the floor.

- Lower your right hand to the mat in front of your left foot, and stretch your left hand toward the ceiling, keeping it in line with your right hand.

- Twist from your waist, not your hips. Your head should turn away from your tailbone.

BEGINNER	ADVANCED
Hold the pose for 3 breaths. Perform this pose once on each side.	Hold the pose for 5 breaths. Perform this pose 3 times on each side.

(PASCHIMOTTANASANA)

- Sit on the floor, holding your big toes, with your legs straight out in front of you.

- Bend forward at the hips, and lower your head toward your knees.

- Reach your hands past your feet, and clasp them in front of you if possible.

- Do not tuck your tailbone under, but stay centered on your sit bones.

- Lengthen your spine, and keep your feet flexed.

LEVEL 3: FLOW 2

BEGINNER	ADVANCED
Hold the pose for 3 breaths.	Hold the pose for 5 breaths.

#34 SEATED BOUND HALF LOTUS POSE

(ARDHA BADDHA PADMA PASCHIMOTTANASANA)

- From Seated Forward Bend, bend one knee and tuck the sole of that foot into your opposite inside hip.

- Hold the big toe of the straight leg with your hand, and wrap your other arm around your back to grab the big toe of your bent leg.

- Bend forward at the hips, and lower your head toward your knee.

- Stay centered on your sit bones.

- Lengthen your spine, and keep your feet flexed.

BEGINNER	ADVANCED
Hold the pose for 3 breaths. Perform this pose once on each side.	Hold the pose for 5 breaths. Perform this pose 3 times on each side.

#35 SIDE STRETCH IN HALF HERO POSE

(PARIGHASANA VARIATION)

- Sit upright, with one leg straight out to the side and the other with the knee bent and the foot behind you.

- Keeping the foot and knee of your straight leg pointing to the ceiling, raise one arm up over your head and reach sideways to your opposite foot.

- Place your other arm on the floor in front or tucked in against the inner thigh of your straight leg.

- Lengthen out from your lower back.

BEGINNER	ADVANCED
Hold the pose for 3 breaths. Perform this pose once on each side.	Hold the pose for 5 breaths. Perform this pose 3 times on each side.

#36 HERO POSE

(VIRASANA)

- Kneel on the floor with your feet to the sides of your hips and the tops of your feet flat on the mat.

- Place your hands on your thighs, palms up, and sit completely upright while looking forward.

BEGINNER	ADVANCED
Hold the pose for 3 breaths.	Hold the pose for 5 breaths.

(SETU BANDHASANA)

HALF BRIDGE

- Lie flat on your back, with your knees bent, your feet flat on the mat and slightly apart, and your arms by your sides.

- Inhale and lift your hips off the mat, rolling up onto your shoulders and into a back bend.

- Bring your arms straight under your torso, clasping your hands together between your feet.

FULL BRIDGE

- Lie on your back on the mat, with your knees bent and your feet flat, about hip-width apart.

- Place your hands flat on the floor to the sides of your head with your fingers pointing toward your feet.

- Exhale and press your hands into the floor, lifting your hips, shoulders, and head.

- Straighten your arms and drop your head to look toward the floor.

BEGINNER	ADVANCED
Hold each pose for 3 breaths.	Hold each pose for 5 breaths.

#38 SHOULDER STAND VARIATION

(SARVANGASANA)

- From Full Bridge, lower yourself back to the floor to lie flat.

- Bring your knees to your chest and feet overhead as if going into Plow pose.

- Press your arms into the floor.

- Bend your elbows, placing your hands on your lower back to support your body.

- Straighten your legs overhead, lifting your torso off the floor.

- Lower one leg straight down in front toward the floor.

- Return to the upright position, and repeat with the other leg.

BEGINNER	ADVANCED
Hold the pose for 3 breaths. Lower your legs once to each side.	Hold the pose for 5 breaths. Lower your legs 3 times to each side.

#39 RECLINED TWISTS TO CORPSE POSE

(RECLINED TWISTS TO SAVASANA)

RECLINED TWISTS

- Lie on your back, with your legs extended straight out and your arms stretched out to the sides.

- Bring one leg up straight, and then slowly lower it down to the opposite side while keeping the other leg straight.

- Clasp your ankle or calf with your hand to help ease your leg to the mat.

- Turn your head to the opposite side, and look toward the fingers of your outstretched arm.

CORPSE POSE

- Lie flat on your back on the mat, with your legs slightly apart and your arms stretched out by your sides, palms up.

- Close your eyes and relax your breathing, letting go of any tension.

BEGINNER	ADVANCED
Hold Reclined Twists for 3 breaths. Perform Reclined Twists once on each side before going into Corpse Pose. Hold Corpse Pose for a few minutes.	Hold Reclined Twists for 5 breaths. Perform Reclined Twists 3 times on each side before going into Corpse Pose. Hold Corpse Pose for a few minutes.

INDEX

ABOUT THE AUTHOR

DECLAN CONDRON, MS, CSCS, USAW

Declan has been in the fitness industry for over ten years. He has worked as a Strength and Conditioning Coach, Physical Education Instructor, and Personal Trainer. As an elite personal trainer at an exclusive New York City gym, Declan has held the positions of Personal Training Manager, Fitness Manager, and Personal Trainer.

Declan holds a M.S. and B.S. degree in Exercise Physiology from Southern Connecticut State University and Hofstra University respectively. He is a Certified Strength and Conditioning Specialist (CSCS) through the National Strength and Conditioning Association (NSCA).

As co-founder and fitness expert for PumpOne®, the portable personal training program for color image-ready handheld devices like the iPod, nano Treo, and more, Declan has designed all the custom workouts for consumers with varying fitness level and needs.

PUMPONE®

Created from the belief that clear exercise photography accompanied by concise tips will make a user-friendly exercise program, Craig Schlossberg and Declan Condron founded PumpOne to help you reach your fitness goals through complete intensity-guided workouts. Declan's expert fitness programs coupled with Craig's digital imagery have spawned a multi-media fitness product line that is available on the web at: http://www.PumpOne.com and at retailers nationwide.